P9-EED-841

Dear God Kids®

WORDS AND MEANINGS

by Annie Fitzgerald

A LITTLE SIMON BOOK
PUBLISHED BY SIMON & SCHUSTER, INC., NEW YORK

Dear God,

Today I learned to write your name
beginning with a G
and then I drew a big round O
and finished it with D.

Annie

Dear God,

Some words I like to hear
but others make me sad.
I like to hear the letter G
in garden, God and glad.

Dear God,

MY BROTHER HAS SOME BLOCKS
WITH LETTERS ON EACH SIDE.
HE'S MADE A WORD CALLED NGRBOJ,
OH WELL, AT LEAST HE TRIED.

Dear God,

When I've said something wrong,
or even something rude,
mom says I have to eat my words,
but I'd prefer some food!

Dear God,

aren't letters funny things ?
were they your idea ?
you might have made them easier
for all us kids down here.

Dear God,

can you spell **DIFFICULT** ?
and has it got two i's ?
I know I'm meant to know myself,
but you are truly wise.

Annie

Dear God,

what is the longest word ?
I'm sure that you can tell it.
I know I don't know what it is,
I certainly can't spell it!

Dear God,

How far is ever?
It's further than the sky.
It's hard to reach that far, I know,
but I can, if I try.

Dear God,

HOW DO YOU MAKE CLOUDS
SO WHITE AND SOFT AND FLUFFY ?
THEY FLOAT ACROSS THE SKY ALL DAY
AND NEVER SEEM TO WORRY.

Dear God,

WINTER IS THE TIME FOR SNOW,
AND IT COMES WITHOUT MUCH WARNING.
THEN YOU SEND A BIT OF SUN
AND IT'S GONE AGAIN NEXT MORNING.

Dear God,

YOU'LL THINK ME SILLY,
BUT I CAN'T WRITE MY NAME.
I TRY TO WRITE IT, BUT THE WORDS
JUST DON'T COME OUT THE SAME !

Dear God,

Some words are very big
and others very small.
It's hard to know which ones to use,
so I just try them all.

Dear God,

PLEASE HELP ME READ THIS BOOK,
IT'S VERY THICK, IT'S TRUE.
IT'S FULL OF LOTS OF BIG WORDS, BUT
I ONLY KNOW a few.

Dear God,

at school when teacher says
"today we learn to spell."
suddenly, out of the blue,
I don't feel very well.

Dear God,

Do you like teachers?
Or do you like me best?
If you like me, I wonder if
you'd stop her spelling tests.

Dear God,

MY MOM'S BIG SISTER'S COMING SOON,
IT'S JUST A WEEKEND VISIT.
I'VE WRITTEN **HELO ANTY**
BUT I DON'T THINK THAT'S RIGHT, IS IT?

Dear God,

Holidays mean lots of sun...
Please make it shine this minute,
because we've got a backyard lounge
and I am lying in it.

Dear God,

I love this world that you have made,
and all the things I see.
There's one more thing I'd like to add—
I'm glad that you made me.

Dear God,

WHO MADE THE SEA AND SKY
AND ALL THINGS THROUGH THE AGES,
THERE'S SOMETHING THAT YOU OUGHT TO KNOW,
YOU'RE NOT IN THE YELLOW PAGES.

This book was devised and produced by
Multimedia Publications (UK) Ltd.

Illustrations copyright © 1984 INTERCONTINENTAL GREETINGS LTD
Illustrations by Annie Fitzgerald
Text copyright © 1984 Roger Knights
This edition copyright © 1984 Multimedia Publications (UK) Ltd.
All rights reserved including the right of
reproduction in whole or in part in any form.

First published in the United States of America 1985 by
LITTLE SIMON, a division of Simon & Schuster, Inc.,
1230 Avenue of Americas, New York, New York 10020.
LITTLE SIMON and colophon are registered
trademarks of Simon & Schuster, Inc.

DEAR GOD KIDS is a registered trademark
of Intercontinental Greetings, New York.

ISBN 0-671-54679-1

Originated by D.S. Colour International Ltd.
Printed in Italy by New Interlitho.